MEANINGFUL PLAYTIME

A science-based guide for quality play with your child

By

Maria Machi

Grosvenor House
Publishing Limited

This book is published by
Grosvenor House Publishing Ltd
Link House
140 The Broadway, Tolworth, Surrey, KT6 7HT.
www.grosvenorhousepublishing.co.uk

A CIP record for this book
is available from the British Library

ISBN 978-1-80381-848-1
eBook ISBN 978-1-80381-849-8

Contents

Important disclaimer

The information and advice provided in this book are intended solely for informational and educational purposes and should not be considered as medical or psychological advice. This content is not a substitute for professional medical or psychological consultation, diagnosis, or treatment.

As the author, I emphasise the importance of consulting qualified health professionals for any concerns regarding a child's developmental, psychological, or medical well-being. Do not ignore or delay seeking professional advice based on information read in this book.

This book is specifically not intended to address severe psychological or medical issues. If you encounter a mental health emergency or medical crisis with your child, it's crucial to seek immediate medical assistance. While the Meaningful Playtime concepts we discuss are designed to enrich children's play experiences and foster emotional and psychological growth, they are not substitutes for professional intervention in cases of complex developmental or psychological challenges.

I do not assume responsibility for any issues that may arise after applying the methods described in this book. If challenges or concerns develop, professional guidance should always be sought. The book's purpose is to inform and suggest ways to enhance the benefits of play for children, not to provide comprehensive solutions for serious concerns.

Preface

As a psychologist and a play therapist, I've dedicated my professional life to understanding and fostering the extraordinary world of children's play. My journey began with a deep curiosity about how young minds develop through play, and this led me to pursue a career where I could explore and facilitate this crucial aspect of childhood. My career has led me to collaborate with leading institutions across Europe dedicated to child psychotherapy and wellbeing. Engaging with diverse teams and theories in these settings has greatly enriched my understanding and approach to play therapy.

In my private practice, I have encountered a wide range of personal stories, each revealing unique insights into the world of children's emotions and imaginations. These experiences have not only deepened my passion for this field but have also shaped my belief in the transformative power of play. I firmly believe that every child deserves plenty of time for play, and it's crucial for parents to not only observe but also participate in this wonderful world of growth and discovery.

Throughout my career, I've noticed a gap in accessible resources for parents and caregivers about the importance of play. This realization led to the beginning of this book, a turning point marking a period of profound personal and professional growth. I began crafting a simple, accessible guide, initially intended as a personal project for close friends and clients. Its goal was to demystify the essence of play, highlight its significant impact on child development, and demonstrate how it can be a powerful tool for parents to strengthen bonds and promote their child's holistic growth.

As the guide took shape, it evolved our understanding and approach to parenting. Witnessing this transformation, my husband suggested an idea: sharing these insights with a broader audience of parents and caregivers. Hence, this book was born. It's a synthesis of theory and practice, designed to be approachable, practical, and transformative. It aims to enlighten, guide, and inspire parents, whether they are new to parenting or have been on this journey for a while. This book is not just about entertainment but about using play as a strategic approach to connect with and empower your child.

Welcome to a journey of discovery, bonding, and joy in the world of play. Together, let's explore how play can be the foundation for a strong, healthy, and joyful childhood, laying the groundwork for a fulfilling adult life.

1. Introduction

Have you ever watched your child absorbed in play, talking to an imaginary friend, or creating a magical world with their toys, and wondered about the strength of their imagination? Play is more than just a way for kids to pass the time. It's an essential tool for a child's development. Every toy, imaginary companion, and story they invent plays a big part in helping them understand the world around them.

Play is a child's fundamental right, recognized by the United Nations as a crucial element of childhood (Office of the United Nations High Commissioner for Human Rights, 1989). In modern life, children are quickly moved into structured academic routines, preparing for adult life from a young age, while parents, busy with the demands of daily routine, find less time to engage in play with their children. Additionally, screens have often taken the place of the imaginative play that used to fill youngsters' time.

But this book isn't about pointing fingers or placing blame. It's the reality – parents are stretched thin, and academic pursuits are undeniably important for child development. This book is instead a call for bringing back the important role of parent-child play in a child's life, trying to balance it with the pressures of modern living.

This book introduces you to key concepts that are usually part of Play Therapy, but in a way that is useful and easy for you as a parent. Play Therapy is a therapeutic approach where play is used as a medium for children to express and process their emotions, thoughts, and experiences. It's based on the understanding that play is a natural form of communication for children, allowing them to explore and make sense of their world in a safe environment. You'll see how play can be a way for children to share their feelings, thoughts, and experiences in a natural and comfortable way. Through play, children can deal with everything from everyday happiness to more complex emotions. It becomes their safe place and their natural way of exploring and expressing themselves. While playing alone is good, involving you – the parent – with insights from Play Therapy approaches makes these experiences even better. This journey isn't about setting up structured playdates or buying the newest toys; it's about making your relationship with your child stronger, helping them grow, and improving how you communicate with each other.

Throughout the book, you'll find Virginia Axline's Play Therapy principles turned into practical, parent-friendly methods. Axline, a renowned psychologist, is best known for developing non-directive Play Therapy. This guide will help you create Meaningful Playtime sessions, a designated weekly time where you'll apply the Play Therapy techniques learned from this book to enrich your interactions with your child and empower their overall development. This approach isn't about fixing problems but using play as a proactive way to support wellbeing and development, similar to the way adults use yoga or mindfulness for their well-being. Axline's work primarily focuses on allowing children to lead in play sessions. Her impactful principles, often hidden in academic books, are made easy and useful for you in this book. By making time for Meaningful Playtime sessions, you're not just entertaining your child; you're actively helping them grow, setting the foundation for a happy, well-rounded childhood.

Whether your goal is to make your bond stronger, support your child in facing life's challenges, or simply join them in their world of imagination, this guide offers the insights and tools you need. Let's start this journey to discover the amazing, transformative power of play and its deep impact on our children's lives.

2. What will you and your child gain from Meaningful Playtime sessions?

Participating in playtime with your children is far more than fun; it's an invaluable opportunity to build stronger connections. You might sometimes think that playtime is just for children, perhaps feeling, "My child plays well alone; they don't really need me." However, the impact is much more significant. When you, as a parent or significant adult, join in your child's play, you're not merely entering their world; you're enriching it. This shared activity becomes an emotional bridge, turning moments of isolation or uncertainty into experiences of connection and confidence.

Play provides your children with a unique way to express their deepest feelings and experiences, ones they may not easily voice in day-to-day conversations. They might not directly express feelings like, "I felt left out at school today", but through play they can recreate scenarios that hint at these emotions. Such moments offer you a window into their inner world. When they invite you into their play with a simple, "Want to play with me?" they're seeking more than just your participation; they're asking for your validation and presence. Engaging with them in play is not just about having fun together; it's about affirming their value and importance in your life.

Diving into the world of imaginative play might initially feel awkward or unfamiliar to many adults. But like many skills, it becomes more natural with time and practice. Actively participating in your children's playtime does more than provide entertainment. It creates a nurturing space where children can heal from past upsets, build self-esteem, assimilate new experiences, navigate complex emotions, and strengthen the bond with you. While children naturally turn to play for self-expression and understanding, your involvement enhances this experience, offering them the supportive presence they often seek.

In essence, Meaningful Playtime with your children is a crucial channel for deepening your bond, understanding your child's inner world, and fostering their emotional and social development. This practice allows you to become an integral part of their learning and growth journey. Through play, children communicate their feelings, fears, and joys, feeling seen, heard, and valued. This strengthens their sense of self-worth and confidence. For you, it's an opportunity to rediscover the joy of imaginative play and connect with your child on a profound level. Ultimately, Meaningful Playtime is a powerful tool that nurtures your child's emotional health and fortifies your relationship, laying a strong foundation for their overall well-being and happiness.

3. A few notes before kick-off

Before diving into the heart of meaningful play, I want to share a few insights:

1. In this book, I've included some theoretical background because I believe understanding the basic concepts of play, its various stages and types, can greatly enhance your journey into Meaningful Playtime with your child. However, if you're keen to move directly into practical application, feel free to skip ahead to Sections 8 (Child-centered vs structured play: Crafting the heart of meaningful playtime) and 9 (The ultimate easy step-by-step guide on how to engage in Meaningful Playtime). These sections contain the most essential information you'll need to effectively engage in enriching play experiences with your child.

2. It's important to remember that the guide for Meaningful Playtime shared in this book is ideally suited for children 3 years and above. However, this doesn't mean you can't have Meaningful Playtime with your child before this age. In Section 10, I have included some important tips on how to adapt the principles to engage with babies and toddlers.

3. Another important aspect to keep in mind as you journey through this book is the specific focus on Meaningful Playtime techniques. While these methods

are designed to enhance scheduled Meaningful Playtime sessions with your child, it's important to recognize that they aren't the only way to engage in play. Outside of these sessions, there's a whole world of play types, like games with rules, solo play, social play, and spontaneous play, which are equally valuable and enriching. Engaging in a diverse array of play experiences with your child is beneficial and encouraged. These varied forms of play contribute significantly to your child's social, emotional, and cognitive development. So, while Meaningful Playtime offers important benefits, remember to also embrace and enjoy the wide spectrum of play activities with your child.

4. Please note that all characters and stories used in this book are purely fictional. Any resemblance to actual events or to any real persons, living or deceased, is purely coincidental. The scenarios and examples provided are created for illustrative purposes, to help convey the principles of Play Therapy in a relatable and understandable way.

5. Remember, the strategies and methods discussed are meant to be adaptable to a variety of situations, allowing you to tailor them to your unique parenting journey and your child's individual needs.

6. While this book provides guidance and insights on enriching your child's play experiences, it's crucial to remember that the information presented is not medical or psychological advice. The concepts and strategies discussed are for informational

and educational purposes only and should not substitute professional medical or psychological consultation, especially in dealing with complex developmental or psychological challenges. Always seek professional advice for specific concerns about your child's well-being.

4. What is play?

As we embark on this journey to understand the transformative power of play, it's crucial first to define what "play" truly means. Drawing from the insights of Garvey (1977), we can explore the essence of play through these guiding principles:

1. **Play is pleasurable and enjoyable:**
    At its core, play is about joy. It's those moments when you see your child's eyes light up, hear their infectious laughter, and witness their uninhibited delight.

2. **Play has no extrinsic goals:**
    Children don't play with a specific outcome in mind. They're not driven by external rewards or achievements. Instead, play is about living in the present, fully immersing in the joy of the moment.

3. **Play is spontaneous and voluntary:**
    True play isn't scripted. It flows naturally, stemming from a child's innate curiosity and creativity. It's never forced; it's always genuine and voluntary, bursting forth when the child feels the urge.

4. **Play involves active engagement:**
    Play isn't passive. It demands active involvement, both mentally and physically. It isn't merely a way to

kill time but a passionate dive into a world of exploration and excitement.

5. **Play contains an element of make-believe:**
    Imagination is the heart of play. It's in those magical moments when everyday objects transform in the hands of a child – a simple stick becomes a wizard's wand, and a blanket into a superhero's cape.

With these principles as our foundation, we can better appreciate the myriad ways play manifests in a child's life and how, as caregivers, we can foster and engage in this natural form of expression.

5. What are the functions of play?

1. Play helps children navigate and comprehend their world

Play serves as a powerful tool in helping children navigate and comprehend the vast world around them. Through play, children can simulate different scenarios, thereby gaining a deeper understanding of various situations and acquiring a sense of empowerment over their lives. It's more than just fun; it's a mechanism for understanding and growth.

For example, as adults, many of us look for breaks or quiet moments to clear our heads. We all know how stress can make it hard to think. Consider when someone is explaining the steps for a new and complicated task at work, like a new accounting procedure with multiple stages. It can quickly become overwhelming. Sometimes, we just want to be alone to go over the steps slowly and figure it out at our own pace. These quiet moments help us sort through information and tackle the task with clarity.

Similarly, children try to understand the world around them. However, their primary way of deciphering complex situations and learning about their environment is through play. Whether it's through role-playing, building structures, or experimenting with toys, children recreate the scenarios they've encountered in their lives. By doing so, they can take in new information, explore cause-and-effect relationships, and even practice problem-solving skills. This practice empowers them to feel confident as they face the real-world situations that inspired their play in the first place.

Let's see an example:

Sophia, a six-year-old, recently visited a local fire station on a school trip. The experience was filled with awe and wonder as she watched firefighters slide down poles, witnessed the blaring sirens, and even got to sit in the firetruck. It was a day filled with new sights, sounds, and a lot of information.

A few days later, at home, her parents noticed her gathering red toy blocks, her toy doll, and some toy figures. In her play area, Sophia began building what looked like a fire station out of her blocks. She then started to enact a scene where one of her toy figures, representing a firefighter, 'rescued' her doll from a 'fire'. She used a string as the fire pole and even imitated the siren sound she had heard during her trip.

Through this play, Sophia was not just remembering her visit to the fire station. She was actively processing everything she had learned. By recreating the scene, she understood the roles of the firefighters, the purpose of the loud sirens, and the quick actions required during emergencies. Her play allowed her to explore the cause-and-effect relationship – when there's a fire, the siren goes off, and the firefighters come to the rescue. Furthermore, by being in charge of this play scenario, Sophia felt empowered, practicing the problem-solving she had observed, and confidently navigating a complex situation on her own terms.

2. Play acts as a therapeutic medium for integrating feelings and emotions

Children use play as a means to navigate adversity and comprehend challenging experiences. When words fall short, they turn to play as a means to integrate feelings. Toys become an extension of their emotions, allowing them to showcase worries, dreams, and even guilt, without directing these feelings at themselves or others. This creates a safe emotional distance, ensuring they're not consumed by their own emotions since it all happens in the realm of make-believe. Through reenacting and sometimes altering distressing scenarios in play, children find a path towards inner peace, gaining the tools they need to navigate and adjust to life's challenges (Landreth, 1993). By reenacting or narrating these scenarios, children can reshape the narrative, placing themselves in control, which paves the way for emotional recuperation.

Therefore, through the safe haven of play, children find a space to heal and regain their equilibrium. Instead of just thinking about things as adults might, children act out their thoughts and feelings through their games and stories. McMahon (2009: 6) mentioned that "in pretend play children can safely bash, bury and throw away the people they are angry with or frightened of or re-enact something that has happened, perhaps changing the outcome." Similarly, Erikson (1965: 214-215) believed that when children are upset, play is their way of working things out, stating that children approach play with "whatever aspect of his ego has been ruffled most... To play it out is the most natural self-healing method childhood affords." Landreth (1993) stated that "play is the child's symbolic language of self-expression, and for children to play out their experiences and feelings is the most natural, dynamic, and self-healing process in which they can engage".

Let's see an example:

James, an eight-year-old boy, was always a bubbly and enthusiastic student. However, recently he started exhibiting signs of anxiety and hesitation, especially when it was time to go to school. His teachers noticed a decline in his participation, and his parents became increasingly concerned after James complained of stomach aches every morning.

Trying to uncover the root cause, his parents realized that James was being teased on the bus by some older students. They were calling him names and making fun of his new glasses. James felt humiliated and dreaded the bus ride every day.

A few days later, his mother walked into his room to find James engrossed in setting up a scene with his toy animals. The 'lion' with spectacles was surrounded by a group of 'hyenas' that seemed to be laughing and pointing at the lion. However, as she watched, James introduced an 'elephant' who came to the lion's defense, addressing the hyenas about the importance of kindness and the uniqueness of everyone. The lion, though initially downcast, soon stood tall with the help of the elephant, and the scene ended with all the animals playing harmoniously together.

Through this play, James was clearly working through his feelings regarding the teasing. The lion, symbolizing James, felt isolated and ridiculed. The elephant, a figure of strength and wisdom, possibly representing a desired ally or a protective figure like a teacher or parent, stepped in to rectify the situation. By making the animals reconcile in the end, James was expressing a hopeful outcome: that the teasing would stop, and he could feel accepted and comfortable again.

This imaginative play allowed James to process his feelings of humiliation and isolation. It gave him a controlled environment to confront his anxieties and visualize a more positive outcome. Through the scenarios he enacted, he was slowly building the resilience and hope needed to face the real-world challenge.

3. Play is a way of communication

Beyond its therapeutic value and its role in helping children navigate their surroundings, play is a pivotal form of communication for them. This is especially crucial for younger children who might not yet have the linguistic skills to express complex feelings or situations.

The scenarios they create, the toys they gravitate towards, and the roles they assume during play can speak volumes about their internal world.

For caregivers, understanding this language of play can be incredibly enlightening. Patterns in play can shine a light on persistent thoughts or concerns. For instance, a child consistently sidelining a particular toy could be emblematic of feelings of exclusion or isolation. On the other hand, frequent themes of rescue or protection in their narratives might hint at a desire for security or a way to process experiences of vulnerability.

In this light, play can be seen as a dialogue. By paying attention to it, parents and caregivers can gain profound insights, facilitating more empathetic and effective communication with the child.

Let's see an example:

Isabella, a five-year-old girl, had always been the center of attention in her family. Recently, her world had been turned upside down when her parents brought home a new baby brother. At first, she appeared excited, talking about the baby and asking questions. But as days turned into weeks, her enthusiasm seemed to wane.

During her daily play sessions, Isabella's parents observed how she had recently started to use her dollhouse to create family scenarios. In the heart of the dollhouse, a tiny infant doll took the center stage, with dolls representing other family members constantly hovering around, attending to the baby's needs. Interestingly, a doll that resembled Isabella, was often placed in an upstairs room, away from the main activities, peering out from a tiny window.

One day, Isabella's mother, seeing this pattern, decided to join her during playtime. Taking another doll, she engaged in a dialogue with the Isabella-like doll, asking, "Why are you up here by yourself? Don't you want to join the others downstairs?" Through the dolls, Isabella began to communicate her feelings of being left out and her worries that her parents might not love her as much anymore.

This play session provided a valuable opportunity for Isabella's mother to reassure her, explaining that while the new baby needs care due to his age, it doesn't diminish the immense love they have for her.

4. Play serves as an avenue for intrinsic learning

Having explored play's roles in helping children comprehend their world, process emotions, and foster communication, we now turn our attention to yet another pivotal function of play – its capacity to facilitate intrinsic learning. Unlike the structured environment of traditional classrooms, the world of play serves as a spontaneous and dynamic setting where learning happens organically.

When children engage in play, several cognitive processes come into action. Firstly, they practice decision-making and problem-solving. For example, a child building with blocks decides where to place each piece, and if the tower falls, they learn to reconsider their approach.

Moreover, through imaginative scenarios, kids develop their narrative skills, honing their ability to sequence events logically and understanding cause and effect. They might stage a doll's birthday party, sequentially planning the invitation, decorations, and the cake cutting, thereby grasping the concept of events unfolding in a particular order.

Children also cultivate their social and emotional skills through play. By negotiating roles in a pretend game or waiting their turn on the swing, they learn the nuances of cooperation, sharing, and understanding others' perspectives.

Play also offers ample opportunities for children to practice and reinforce academic skills. A simple game of shop involves math as they "buy" and "sell" items, literacy as they "read" product labels, and even science when they weigh produce on a scale.

Lastly, the hands-on nature of play enhances fine and gross motor skills. Whether it's manipulating tiny beads for a craft or hopping across the playground, children hone their physical abilities, which further aids their cognitive development.

Each playful interaction not only entertains but is rife with educational undertones, equipping children with an understanding that seamlessly bridges their imaginative realm with real-world complexities.

Let's see an example:

At eight years old, Max loved to play "toy shop" with his younger sister, Lily. Using his toys and books as items for sale, he would assign each a price tag, often ranging from 1 to 50 cents. Lily would come as a customer, picking out items she wanted to "buy".

During their play, Max used a toy cash register to calculate the total cost of the items Lily chose. For instance, if she picked up a toy car priced at 20 cents and a book priced at 30 cents, Max would mentally add the amounts, stating the total as 50 cents. Lily would then hand over her play money, and Max would determine the correct change to give back if she handed over more than the total cost.

With every transaction, Max practiced basic addition and subtraction. He also began grasping concepts like estimation when he'd try to round up prices or provide discounts. Their play sessions became a fun, interactive way for Max to hone his math skills, all while engaging in a game with his sister.

In wrapping up our exploration on the functions of play, it's undeniable that play is the foundation of a child's cognitive, emotional, and social development. Through the diverse realms of play, children embark on journeys of self-discovery and knowledge acquisition, consistently challenging and expanding their understanding of the world. The playful scenarios, seemingly simple, are in fact rehearsals for reality. They allow children to grapple with multifaceted emotions, confront fears, and explore various roles, all within a secure, controlled environment. Whether it's through mimicking adult roles in pretend games, constructing intricate buildings, or simply conversing with their toys, kids craft stories that not only entertain but also enlighten. This is their way of turning the unknown into the familiar, the feared into the understood. Hence, play is not just leisure; it's a child's bridge to comprehension, resilience, and empowerment. As caregivers and observers, it is imperative to recognize and value this instinctive medium, ensuring children have sufficient opportunities to immerse themselves in the transformative power of play.

6. Stages of play

To understand how children's play progresses as they age, we look to Jean Piaget's (1951) insights. He identified key stages in a child's development, each characterized by a distinct type of play.

Before delving deeper into these stages, there are three important notes to consider:

1. When a new play stage emerges, it doesn't replace the previous ones. Instead, the earlier style evolves, becomes more sophisticated, and typically supports the newer form of play.
2. While the order of these play stages remains consistent for all children, the age at which each child enters a particular stage can differ.
3. Constructive play runs in parallel to all the other stages (from year 1).

0-2 years – Functional play

Functional play is about repeatedly performing actions to observe the results. At this stage, children engage in play by exploring with their five senses. For instance, they might shake a rattle to hear its sound or repeatedly touch a fuzzy blanket to feel its softness. They're curious about two primary things: their own bodies and the objects around them. Upon closer observation, starting from about 6 months, these tiny adventurers begin piecing together what they know. New toys might confuse them initially, but soon they'll be exploring and experimenting to understand. As they grow, their play becomes more intentional. A toddler might pretend to chat on a toy phone, mimicking Mom's daily calls or try to "cook" with play pots and pans after observing dinner preparations. It's not just about reactions anymore; it's about predicting outcomes and laying the groundwork for imaginative play to become central.

Benefits of functional play

1. **Sensory development:** During functional play, children actively engage with their surroundings, providing a rich opportunity for sensory exploration. By touching different materials, like the smooth surface of a wooden block or the soft texture of a stuffed animal, they enhance their tactile experiences. They may shake toys to listen to any sounds or even bring them close to their nose to discern any smells. Observing the varied colors and shapes of toys aids their visual development. For instance, when a child repeatedly drops a rubber ball just to see it bounce and hear the thud, they are actively engaging multiple senses, thereby deepening their sensory understanding. Through these simple actions, they immerse themselves fully in the world of play, refining their sensory perceptions.

2. **Hand-eye coordination:** At this stage of development, children focus on the vital skill of aligning what they see with how they move their hands. This coordination

is developed through various play activities. For example, when a child attempts to fit a square block into a matching hole or tries to catch a rolling toy, they are practicing and enhancing their hand-eye coordination. Activities such as manipulating toys, picking up and placing objects, or even the simple act of stacking one toy on top of another, all contribute to refining this essential skill. This coordination not only aids in play but also prepares them for more complex tasks they'll encounter as they grow.

3. **Understanding the world:** During functional play, babies begin to comprehend some fundamental aspects of their environment:

Object permanence: This concept means that even when an object is out of their line of sight, it still exists. For example, if you hide a toy behind your back and it seemingly "disappears", a baby gradually learns that the toy hasn't vanished but is merely hidden.

Cause and effect: As babies play, they start to recognize that specific actions produce predictable results. For instance, when they push a toy car, it moves; when they shake a rattle, it makes a sound. These simple interactions help them understand the cause-and-effect principle inherent in their surroundings.

Combination of items: Babies discover that they can mix and match different toys or items to create new experiences or reactions. A simple instance might be combining colored blocks to form patterns or merging different shapes to make a structure.

4. **Movement coordination:** Through play, children fine-tune the coordination of their movements, aiding them in achieving specific tasks. For example, a child might learn to expertly crawl or toddle towards a distant toy, overcoming obstacles in their path. Similarly, as they engage with different toys, they start discerning varying textures, shapes, and functionalities, adapting their grip and touch accordingly. This coordinated movement not only enhances their physical skills but also boosts their curiosity and exploration of the world around them.

5. **Static and dynamic balance:** Playtime serves as a crucial platform for children to develop their sense of balance. In the midst of their play, they acquire the ability to maintain stability. For instance, when standing or sitting without moving (static balance), they learn to hold their posture. Conversely, when they're in motion, like running or hopping (dynamic balance), they understand how to adjust their bodies to prevent tumbling. This mastery over balance is essential not only for their current play activities but also as a foundational skill for future physical tasks.

6. **Self-improvement:** At the heart of a child's nature is an inherent desire to learn and improve. During functional play, they naturally dissect the world around them, spotting recurring patterns and tweaking their approaches accordingly. For example,

a child might adjust the way they stack blocks after noticing a particular method causes them to topple. Each new discovery or slight improvement in their play actions becomes a source of joy and pride, further fueling their thirst for knowledge and skill enhancement.

7. **Social Interaction:** Even though functional play often seems like a solo activity, it lays the foundational bricks for budding social interactions. At this stage, caregivers, parents, older siblings, cousins and so on, often step into the role of the child's first playmates. They not only participate in the play but also offer valuable insights, directions, and context. For example, while a child might be engrossed in banging a spoon on a table, a caregiver can join in, introducing rhythms or turns, transforming a solitary act into an interactive experience. This shared playtime becomes a significant avenue for children to begin understanding the basics of social behavior and collaboration.

From 1 year – Constructive play

Constructive play begins around the age of one and runs concurrently with other play types, evolving as children grow and develop. This play centers on children actively manipulating and crafting with materials to produce or create something. As children mold, build, and arrange, they further their comprehension of various concepts. They pose questions, assess ideas, and gather understanding. Their hands-on encounters with diverse tools, like blocks or Lego, offer them opportunities to strategize, explore, and discover new findings. It's a play form that invites the use of materials ranging from sand, clay, and paint, to cardboard, fabric, and wooden sticks. Each of these materials serves a particular purpose in the child's mission to create, innovate, and realize their visions.

Benefits of constructive play

1. **Boosts creativity:** When children immerse themselves in constructive play, they unlock a world of boundless imagination. Picture a child who takes a few simple wooden blocks and crafts a unique castle with soaring towers, or another who uses colorful clay to sculpt a vibrant garden of flowers, each with its own distinct shape and size. These activities not only give them the freedom to explore different design possibilities but also encourage them to think outside the box. Over time, this helps nurture their innate creative potential, allowing them to visualize and then manifest their innovative concepts into tangible creations.

2. **Enhances social interactions:** Constructive play becomes a communal effort when children team up with their peers. Imagine a group of kids working together to build a sprawling cityscape out of Lego or collaborating on a mural using paint and brushes. These shared experiences foster communication, require compromise, and teach the value of pooling ideas to achieve a common goal. As children negotiate designs or divide up tasks, they not only create a

tangible project but also strengthen bonds and cultivate crucial social skills that will serve them well in future group settings.

3. **Advances hand-eye coordination:** When children embark on projects like stacking blocks to build a tall tower or meticulously connecting puzzle pieces to complete an image, they're honing the fine-tuned dance between what they see and how they respond with their hands. Every successful placement of a Lego piece or threading of a bead onto a string reinforces their ability to interpret visual information and translate it into precise hand movements. Over time this continuous feedback loop improves their coordination, setting the stage for a wide range of activities that require dexterity and visual accuracy, from writing to playing sports.

4. **Improves bodily control:** As children delve into constructive play, they're often faced with tasks that challenge their physical stability and precision. For instance, when they mold clay into a specific shape, they must apply just the right amount of pressure. Similarly, when they're creating a structure with building blocks, they need to exercise restraint and balance to prevent it from toppling over. Each of these activities requires a keen sense of how their body moves and the ability to adjust their actions accordingly. Over time these repeated experiences enhance their overall physical control, helping them navigate other activities with grace and confidence.

5. **Hones fine motor skills:** In the world of constructive play, children are constantly interacting with objects that require delicate handling. Whether it's stringing beads to make a necklace, carefully placing tiny Lego pieces together to craft a masterpiece, or meticulously drawing a design using colored pencils, these tasks all demand precision. As children engage in these detailed activities, the muscles in their fingers and hands get a workout. Over time, with repetition, their agility and dexterity improve, enabling them to take on even more intricate projects with ease and also aiding in everyday tasks like buttoning a shirt or tying shoelaces.

6. **Strengthens attention span:** Constructing a tower out of blocks or designing a complex pattern requires children to pay close attention to their work. They must ensure each piece fits perfectly, and one wrong move could topple their creation. For example, when they're building a house with wooden blocks, they need to think about the foundation, ensure the blocks are aligned, and decide which piece comes next.

7. **Stimulates memory:** Constructive play demands that children recall specific sequences or designs they've encountered before. For instance, after creating a specific design with Lego, a child might want to recreate it days or even weeks later. To do so, they'll have to remember the pattern, the colors used, and the exact sequence they followed. This repeated act of recalling and implementing patterns and sequences aids in strengthening their memory.

8. **Encourages spatial reasoning:** As children build and experiment with three-dimensional objects during constructive play, they gain a deeper comprehension of space, dimensions, and relationships between objects. For example, when assembling a puzzle or building a multi-level structure with blocks, kids learn to visualize how different pieces fit together and occupy space. This hands-on experience provides them with practical insights into concepts like size, distance, and orientation, enhancing their ability to think spatially.

9. **Fosters flexible thinking:** Through the process of constructive play, children often encounter unexpected challenges or roadblocks. Perhaps a tower of blocks keeps toppling, or a design isn't coming together as envisioned. In such situations, they learn the importance of adaptability. For instance, if a certain block doesn't fit, they might seek out an alternative piece or approach the construction from a different angle. These experiences teach them to think on their feet, adapt their strategies, and be open to altering their initial plans, thereby nurturing a mindset that embraces flexibility and resilience.

10. **Boosts self-esteem and control:** Constructive play offers children a hands-on avenue to shape and control their surroundings, granting them a tangible sense of agency. For instance, when a child sets out to build a bridge using wooden sticks and sees it hold, or crafts a sandcastle that stands tall, the sense of accomplishment is palpable. This not only provides

immediate gratification but also builds long-term confidence. Each success, big or small, reinforces their belief in their abilities. Over time these repeated positive experiences contribute to a robust sense of self-worth and an understanding that they have the capability to influence and shape their environment.

2-7 years – Symbolic play

Symbolic play, as the name suggests, centers around the use of symbols or representations to enact scenarios, characters, and objects that aren't physically there. It's a defining aspect of childhood play.

The onset of symbolic play is earlier than many might think. By around 12 months, you might observe a child using objects to imitate their real-life functions, such as pretending to drink from an empty cup. By 18 months, these young minds begin to copy everyday routines, maybe acting like they're having a conversation on a phone or imitating the way adults care for pets. However, it's after the age of 2 that this kind of play truly blossoms and grows rapidly.

Within this imaginative world, children recreate and reflect on their understanding of the reality they see every day. They embark on a journey to understand their surroundings and figure out their role in it. Such imaginative play does more than entertain; it bolsters a child's sense of identity, enhancing their confidence and independence. On a deeper level, symbolic play becomes a safe haven for them, a place where they can deal with various emotions, from fear and happiness to frustration. The variety and depth of their imaginative play often mirror their diverse experiences, letting them take on roles such as chefs, astronauts, caregivers, and firefighters.

Benefits of symbolic play

1. **Improves the understanding of the world:** Symbolic play, particularly role-playing, allows children to step into different shoes, giving them a firsthand experience of various roles in society. Whether they're playing as doctors, teachers, or parents, they're gaining insights into how these figures think and operate. Through these playful scenarios, they not only grasp the complexities of their surroundings but also appreciate the roles and responsibilities of different members in their community. By exchanging and refining their views about the world during these play sessions, they enhance their understanding and begin to see the world from varied perspectives. This comprehensive understanding helps them in navigating their daily interactions and in building empathy toward others.

2. **Boosts communication skills:** Symbolic play enhances essential communication skills. As children engage in scenarios like "playing doctor" or "running a grocery store", they communicate their thoughts, feelings, and ideas. They begin to express more complex ideas, asking questions and responding in kind, learning the details of effective conversation. Through these playful interactions, children not only

share their imaginative worlds but also understand the importance of listening and expressing themselves clearly.

3. **Prepares the child for reading and writing:** Through symbolic play, children familiarize themselves with the concept of symbols representing real-world items or ideas. For example, when they use a banana as a phone or a cardboard box as a car, they're learning that one thing can stand for another – a foundational understanding for recognizing letters and numbers. This intuitive grasp of symbols and representation naturally prepares them for the eventual tasks of reading and writing, setting a strong foundation for future literacy skills.

4. **Expands vocabulary:** Through various scenarios in symbolic play, children often articulate thoughts, desires, and emotions. For instance, when playing "store", a child might ask for specific items like "apples" or "bread", or when playing "doctor", they might use terms like "stethoscope" or "check-up". Over time these pretend dialogues introduce new words and phrases, thereby expanding their vocabulary. Moreover, the give-and-take nature of role-playing with peers or adults promotes better verbal expression, helping them to frame sentences more effectively and communicate their ideas more clearly.

5. **Boosts imagination:** In the realm of symbolic play, children are not confined by the boundaries of reality. Whether they're venturing into outer space as

astronauts, exploring a jungle teeming with wild animals, or ruling over a magical kingdom, their creative minds are at the forefront. Each pretend scenario they craft showcases their limitless imagination. For instance, a simple cardboard box can transform into a spaceship, a castle, or a hidden treasure chest. This type of play encourages them to think outside the box, fostering creativity and innovative thinking that extends beyond the play session.

6. **Problem solving:** During symbolic play, children often set up scenarios that mirror challenges they've observed in the real world or in their own experiences. Perhaps they're hosting a pretend tea party and run out of "tea", or their toy car gets "stuck" in the mud. By navigating these challenges in their imaginative settings, children actively engage in critical thinking. For example, they might "brew" more tea using pretend water or come up with inventive ways to "rescue" the stuck vehicle. Each of these playful situations provides them with an opportunity to brainstorm solutions, test their ideas, and gain confidence in their ability to tackle challenges, preparing them for real-life problem-solving situations as they grow.

7. **Boosts physical skills:** In symbolic play, children aren't just flexing their imaginations; they're also exercising their bodies. Whether they're "flying" as superheroes, "galloping" as horses, or "climbing" a mountain in their living room, these pretend scenarios require a range of physical actions. For instance, setting up a pretend grocery store might have them

walking, bending, and reaching as they "stock" their shelves. Similarly, pretending to be a doctor involves precise hand movements when "administering" a check-up. These activities not only improve their gross motor skills, like running or jumping, but also fine-tune their finer motor skills, like picking up or manipulating small objects, contributing to their overall physical development.

8. **Improves the capacity for handling emotions:** During symbolic play, children often recreate scenarios that mirror their real-life experiences or emotions. For instance, a child might have a doll "cry" because it's "sad", allowing the child to comfort it. Such actions give children a safe space to process, express, and navigate their own feelings. Additionally, they might take on roles that allow them to experience a wide range of emotions – from a heroic firefighter saving the day to a doctor consoling a worried patient. Through these imaginative scenarios, children not only learn to recognize and name different emotions but also develop strategies to manage and express them in healthy ways. Over time this practice equips them with the emotional tools they need to face real-life situations with resilience and understanding.

7-12 years – Games with rules play

Play that involves specific rules determining how participants should act is called "games with rules". Recognized by Piaget as the last type of play, engaging in these games requires children to have the cognitive ability to understand and remember these rules. They must also showcase self-control, occasionally putting their immediate desires aside to follow the rules of the game. Schools frequently introduce children to these types of games, serving as the first experience for many in structured play. Besides classroom activities, board and card games also belong to this category. Through them, children get acquainted with both the details of cooperation and the aspects of competition.

Benefits of games with rules

1. **Enhances social skills:** Engaging in games with rules offers a practical platform for children to learn key social behaviors. For instance, when playing a board game a child might have to wait patiently for their turn while another player thinks through their move. Similarly, they may experience the thrill of victory when they win a game of checkers or the disappointment of a loss in a card game. Through these experiences, they internalize the significance of patience, the essence of taking turns, and the importance of abiding by established rules.

2. **Boost diverse learning:** Games with rules often cover a broad spectrum of topics and subjects. For example, while playing "Monopoly", children are introduced to concepts of money management, decision-making, and strategy. On the other hand, a game like "Trivial Pursuit" offers them insights into various facts from different domains. These games provide an avenue for children to acquire varied types

of knowledge and hone diverse skills in an engaging manner.

3. **Promote language development:** When engaged in games with rules, children often find themselves in situations where they need to articulate their thoughts, ask questions about the game, or even negotiate certain rules with their peers. For instance, during a card game, they might discuss strategies or clarify rule ambiguities. Such interactions naturally enhance their vocabulary, sentence structure, and overall communication skills. It gives them the opportunity to practice and refine their language abilities in a dynamic setting.

4. **Enhance memory:** As children immerse themselves in games with rules, they are frequently tasked with remembering specific regulations, contemplating past decisions, and strategizing for future moves. For example, in a board game like "Monopoly", a child needs to remember property prices, player agreements, and the effects of certain cards. This consistent mental exercise not only strengthens their short-term recall but also contributes to the development of long-term memory retention. Through repeated play, their ability to recall and apply information becomes more efficient and robust.

5. **Foster reasoning abilities:** When children engage in games with defined rules, they are often faced with situations that require foresight and strategy. For instance, in a game like chess, they must anticipate

their opponent's moves, weigh the consequences of their own potential moves, and decide on the best course of action. This constant process of evaluating scenarios, predicting outcomes, and making decisions on the fly, hones their critical thinking abilities. Over time these games help in cultivating a child's ability to reason logically, analyze different options, and select the most advantageous strategy based on the information at hand.

6. **Strengthen attention span:** Playing games that have a set of specific rules requires children to maintain their concentration and stay engaged for extended periods. For example, in a board game, they need to track the game's progress, remember the rules, and strategize their next moves. This consistent requirement to stay attentive, combined with the intrinsic motivation to win or achieve a goal, helps children in enhancing their ability to focus. Over time engaging in such games can lead to a noticeable improvement in a child's ability to concentrate on tasks, not just in play, but also in academic and other settings.

7. Social interaction in play

While we've delved deep into the evolution of play through Piaget's stages, it's essential to spotlight a crucial component that intersects these stages: social interaction. The dance of social exchange during play is not just a backdrop; it's a fundamental ingredient that shapes the very essence of play itself. As children grow, the way they interact with peers and adults takes on new layers of complexity and depth. These interactions not only enrich their play experiences but also play a crucial role in molding their social, emotional, and cognitive development. This progression isn't arbitrary; children's social interactions during play are deeply rooted in their developmental milestones, evolving methodically and predictably over time.

1. Solitary play

Often witnessed during the functional play stage, solitary play is characterized by children deeply immersed in their own activities, creating a universe that is uniquely theirs. This self-contained style of play isn't indicative of any unwillingness to socialize. Instead, it's a foundational step in their developmental pathway. For instance, you might observe a toddler intently stacking blocks or exploring the texture of a plush toy, seemingly oblivious to kids playing nearby. Such moments signify the child's engagement in solitary play. During this phase, the primary objective for the child is to explore themselves and the world directly around them. By playing alone, they get the freedom to set their own pace, make independent choices, and navigate their curiosities. This uninterrupted exploration not only enhances their understanding of different toys, materials, and sounds, but also nurtures their sense of autonomy and confidence in their abilities.

2. Parallel play

Particularly evident between the ages of 2 and 4, parallel play serves as an intriguing shift in how children relate to others during playtime. When observing kids engaged in this form of play, you might initially think they're playing collaboratively because they're sitting side by side or within close proximity. However, upon closer examination, you'll notice that each child is engrossed in their own activity, rarely merging their play themes. For example, two toddlers might sit adjacent to each other, one building a tower of blocks while the other arranges toy animals in a line. They're not building or arranging together, yet they're contentedly sharing the same space. Even without direct communication or collaboration, this stage is significant in a child's social journey. The subtle glances they cast towards their peers, the occasional mimicking of actions, or the subtle adjustments they make to their own play based on what they witness, all hint at the budding social awareness. Through parallel play, children are laying the groundwork for more complex social interactions, silently learning about peer behaviors, sharing, and the beginnings of cooperative play, all while maintaining their independent play narratives.

3. Cooperative play

Emerging predominantly around age 4, cooperative play signals a transformative moment in a child's journey through social interactions. Gone are the days when they played primarily within the boundaries of their personal imaginative realms. Instead, they now enthusiastically dive into collective adventures, discovering the delights that come from shared imaginative ventures. During cooperative play, interactions aren't just casual exchanges; they evolve into comprehensive dialogues and mutual decision-making processes. For instance, children might collectively create a make-believe "space mission", where they assign roles like astronauts, mission control, or even aliens. In the process, they engage in dynamic discussions about the storyline, delegate tasks, and sometimes even negotiate on the rules and direction of their play. This emphasizes the essential nature of communication in cooperative scenarios. Through these interactions, they inadvertently practice and understand the nuances of compromise, the art of negotiation, and the spirit of teamwork. These experiences not only prepare them for future group tasks and collaborations but also help inculcate key life skills. The decisions they make together, whether about the flow of their imaginative story or the sharing and usage of toys, reflect the early stages of collaborative problem-solving, hinting at the sophisticated social interactions they'll master as they grow.

As we conclude this exploration into the evolution of social play, it's vital to underscore that while these stages typically manifest at characteristic ages, they aren't strictly linear or exclusive. The fluidity of child development means that even as children grow and embrace more socially interactive forms of play, the stage of solitary play never truly disappears. A child might be adept at cooperative play during group scenarios, but when left to their own devices they often revert to solitary play, diving deep into their imaginative realms. It's essential to recognize that solo play, regardless of age, continues to offer invaluable benefits to a child's development. Each play stage, whether undertaken solo or with peers, contributes uniquely to shaping their cognitive, emotional, and social growth. So, while the landscape of play might evolve as children mature, the foundational elements remain ever-relevant, consistently nurturing their ever-expanding horizons.

8. Child-centered vs structured play: Crafting the heart of Meaningful Playtime

Before diving further into the world of play, it's crucial to highlight a distinction you might come across: child-centered play versus structured play. In this book, our emphasis is on understanding and reaping the rewards of child-centered play. That said, it's not a call to neglect or diminish the value of structured play. Every type of play has its own set of benefits and contributes uniquely to a child's growth. Structured play offers its own advantages, and it's essential for children to experience it, too. While our primary focus here will be on child-centered play, understanding both types gives you a broader perspective.

1. Structured play

Structured play, also known as directive play, is a relatively organized approach where the activity's course is mostly predetermined and led by an adult. This could be a therapist, parent, teacher, or another caregiver. These activities usually come with instructions that the child is expected to follow. It's a method frequently used in therapeutic environments to address specific developmental or behavioral objectives. For instance, it can be tailored to help children develop essential skills, such as anger management, social interaction, or fine motor skills.

The benefits of structured play for child development are numerous. To name some, it introduces children to a sense of discipline and routine, helping them understand the value of following instructions and the subsequent outcomes. It also offers a clear framework for children to achieve set goals, boosting their self-esteem when they successfully complete the task. Additionally, structured play can enhance cognitive development by challenging children's problem-solving and critical thinking abilities.

Examples of structured play can range from guided craft activities, where a child might be shown how to create a specific object, to more therapeutic settings where a child might be directed to act out a certain scenario with puppets to address and process specific emotions or situations. Another example could be a board game with set rules that need to be followed, ensuring children learn patience, turn-taking, and strategy. In essence, structured play is a powerful tool in guiding children's development, providing them with clear pathways to explore, learn, and grow.

2. Child-centered play

Child-centered play places the child in the driver's seat, empowering them to steer the course of their play. This means that the child is given the primary role in determining how they play. It's like letting a child be the 'driver' in their play activities, where they decide the direction, pace, and nature of their playtime. This empowerment means that the child chooses what to play with, how to play, and the outcomes of their play. In this approach, adults (parents, caregivers, teachers, or therapists) are more like supportive passengers rather than directors. They provide a safe and nurturing environment but do not dictate how the child should play. Instead, they may join in the play as per the child's invitation or guidance, responding to the child's ideas and preferences.

To understand the essence of child-centered play, we draw from Virginia Axline's ideas, a psychologist known for her groundbreaking work in children's therapy. Axline introduced a special form of Play Therapy that highlights children's natural progression towards growth and self-awareness (Landreth, 1993). She advocated for the healing power of play, encouraging kids to lead their playtime. This method lets them express and process their emotions and experiences, recognizing that their play actions are often fueled by a deeper desire to understand themselves and their surroundings. Her approach is rooted in the belief that children learn and grow best when they are free to play in ways that they find meaningful and enjoyable.

Throughout this guide, we'll use Axline's insights as a roadmap. Her approach is a supportive and warm way to help your child's emotional and psychological development. It's incredibly beneficial for you, as a parent, offering a pathway to strengthen and deepen your bond with your child through play. By grasping and implementing these concepts, you can foster an environment where your child is encouraged to explore, express themselves, and grow. I aim to translate Axline's principles into practical strategies for you – the parents and caregivers – to enhance your child's play experiences. Significantly, Axline's non-directive approach suggests that children are inherently capable and motivated to face their own challenges, preferring mature responses to immature ones (Axline, 1947).

Before diving into Axline's principles in detail, it's helpful to understand the three core components of meaningful play as outlined by McMahon (2009), which resonate with the essence of child-centered play:

1. **Safe environment:** Children need a safe space, both physically and emotionally. This means having a designated area and time for play where the usual rules are relaxed, whether or not an adult is involved.

2. **Being in control:** It's vital for children to feel they can direct their play, whether they are playing alone or with others.

3. **Room to experiment:** Play is about exploration. Children should be free to make mistakes without fear of harsh consequences, creating a space where they can try new things, be creative, and learn from their experiences.

Axline's principles

As touched upon earlier, Axline's principles are key to understanding the richness and possibilities of child-centered play. Axline believed that every person, especially children, naturally seeks growth and self-direction (Axline, 1947). This belief is at the heart of her approach, highlighting a child's deep-rooted journey toward self-discovery. For example, a child who often pretends to be a doctor might be working through a personal experience from a visit to the doctor's office. They use play as a tool to understand and come to terms with that experience. Another child might enjoy building elaborate structures with blocks, not just for fun but as a way to practice problem-solving and understand concepts like stability and balance. Axline had great faith in children's ability to tackle their own challenges. Take, for example, a child learning to take turns with friends during a game. This situation isn't just about playing a game; it's about developing social skills and showing a preference for cooperation and understanding rather than conflict. In the following sections, we'll dive deeper into these principles. My goal is to help you, as parents and caregivers, to apply these insights in everyday life, enriching your child's playtime and supporting their growth and learning.

The benefits of applying Axline's principles in Meaningful Playtime with your child

When you incorporate Axline's principles into playtime with your child, you're supporting them in a safe and nurturing way as they explore their emotions. Imagine playtime as a story your child is telling. Rather than guessing how the story might go or end, let them lead the way. This approach ensures you don't rush them into dealing with emotions they might not be ready for. By valuing their story and holding back from drawing quick conclusions about their play, you create a secure space for them to express themselves and grow at their own pace.

Playing with your child and letting them guide the play deepens your bond. When your child sees that you're engaged without controlling their play, and when you respect their choices and individuality, it strengthens your relationship. This method also teaches children to take ownership of their feelings, decisions, and the outcomes of their actions. They learn the importance of personal responsibility, free from the pressure to meet external expectations. This understanding is empowering not just during playtime but also in various other areas of their life. By adopting Axline's approach, you're giving your child the tools to articulate and make sense of their feelings, perspectives, and experiences. You're nurturing their resilience, helping them develop effective coping strategies, and improving their understanding of the world around them.

Let's imagine a scenario with eight-year-old Mia. Recently, Mia felt left out when her friends at school didn't include her in their lunchtime game. Confused and hurt, Mia carried this emotional burden home but didn't know how to talk about it. One evening, during a play session with her mother, Mia chose to act out a school scene with her dolls. She had one doll – representing herself – sitting alone, while the other dolls huddled together. Mia's mother, following the principles of child-centered play, didn't jump to conclusions or direct the play. Instead, she simply observed and occasionally mirrored Mia's actions or words, offering a comforting presence. As Mia continued to play, she started to open up about her feelings, expressing through her dolls what she couldn't say directly. This safe and non-judgmental space allowed Mia to process her feelings of exclusion and articulate them in her own time. Through this play, Mia's mother gained insights into Mia's experiences, and Mia began exploring ways to manage her frustration and considered actions that could lead to more positive outcomes in the future. For instance, she thought about actively asking to join the game next time or finding another group of friends to play with. If Mia hadn't had this opportunity to process her feelings through play, the unresolved emotions might have impacted her self-esteem and social interactions. She might have become more withdrawn or anxious in social situations, fearing further rejection. However, by having a supportive space to explore these feelings, empowered by her mother's empathetic presence, Mia began to understand and cope with the situation. She learned that it's okay to feel upset and that she can navigate difficult emotions and find solutions to frustrating situations.

This play session didn't just help Mia process a challenging experience; it also strengthened the bond between her and her mother. Mia learned that her feelings were valid and important, and her mother learned more about Mia's inner world. Together, they used child-centered play to transform a difficult situation into an opportunity for growth and connection.

Understanding the value of Axline's insights, we're now ready to turn these ideas into action. In the upcoming section, I'll guide you, as a parent or caregiver, on how to apply these principles in your Meaningful Playtime interactions with your child, bringing the concept of child-led play to life in your home. I'll structure this section for ease of understanding: each principle will be introduced with its academic name, followed by a brief explanation of how therapists typically use it in Play Therapy. Then, in the next section, we'll provide a practical guide on how you can incorporate these principles into your Meaningful Playtime with your children, making it both enjoyable and beneficial.

Eight principles of Axline's non-directive Play Therapy, and how parents can apply them while playing with their children

Principle 1: The therapist must develop a warm, friendly relationship with the child, in which good rapport is established as soon as possible.

The essence of Axline's first principle is the establishment of a warm, friendly relationship with the child as a fundamental starting point. For a therapist, this means building a bridge of trust and understanding from the earliest interaction, creating an environment where the child feels safe, valued, and free to express themselves. Such an atmosphere is the soil in which the seeds of healing and personal growth are sown, making it an indispensable aspect of successful Play Therapy.

As a parent or caregiver, applying this principle at home brings a special dimension to your relationship with your child. The natural affection and daily interactions you share with your child lay the foundation for a strong connection. However, it's important to remember that just having a relationship doesn't automatically mean you deeply connect in all areas, especially in play. Play can be a window into your child's inner world.

To truly embrace this principle during playtime, consider setting aside uninterrupted time specifically for playing with your child. It means making a conscious effort to be there both physically and emotionally. Whether your child is building a towering structure from blocks, dressing up as their favorite superhero, or drawing a family portrait, your role is to listen actively and show genuine interest in what they're doing. Small gestures of acknowledgment, like a nod, a smile, or a word of encouragement, can profoundly enhance your child's feeling of being seen and understood. This attention creates a safe space for them, where they feel valued and supported in their explorations and expressions.

Application example:

Imagine your child is absorbed in building a complex structure with their building blocks. Applying this principle, you would join them on the floor, note the colors they choose, and commend their creativity, without taking over the process. Your role is not to direct but to support and appreciate their efforts. As your child notices your genuine interest, not in directing the play but in understanding and appreciating their creations, it reinforces their sense of security and worth. This interaction is not only about the blocks; it's an unspoken conversation, telling your child that their thoughts and feelings are important and that you are a reliable ally in their explorations. This, in turn, sets a solid foundation for deeper connections and more meaningful play experiences.

Principle 2: The therapist accepts the child exactly as they are.

In the therapeutic setting, this principle calls for absolute acceptance of the child by the therapist. It's vital for the therapist to offer a nonjudgmental presence, creating a space where children can express their feelings and thoughts freely. The therapist actively listens and responds to the child in a way that is devoid of evaluation or bias, affirming the child's worth and autonomy. This unconditional acceptance encourages the child to explore their own identity and experiences without fear of criticism or the need for external approval.

For you as a parent, applying this principle at home means embracing your child's uniqueness without passing judgment. It involves observing without directing, listening without interrupting, and understanding without evaluating. This kind of support can help your child feel valued and accepted for who they are, which is critical to their self-esteem and confidence. In practice, this means you offer a supportive presence that acknowledges your child's experiences without overlapping your own expectations or desires.

Application example:

Imagine that your child is quiet and introspective, often engrossed in solo play, creating complex stories with their toys. In this situation, embracing the principle of unconditional acceptance means recognizing and valuing your child as he is. Instead of urging them to be more outgoing or to play in a conventional manner, you can offer a quiet presence, sitting nearby without intruding. You might comment softly, "I see you enjoy playing by yourself and embarking on a big adventure with your toys." This approach validates your child's inner world and mode of play. It shows your respect for their individuality, fostering their self-esteem by affirmatively acknowledging their quiet, thoughtful nature.

Principle 3: The therapist establishes a feeling of permissiveness in the relationship so that the child feels free to express his feelings completely.

In therapy, creating a permissive atmosphere is foundational to the child's emotional expression. This is not about encouraging any behavior but about accepting the full range of the child's emotional experiences. The therapist's role is to provide a secure environment where the child feels free to project their inner feelings onto their play without fear of censure. Whether through robust play, quiet contemplation, or direct verbalization, every action is seen as a meaningful communication of their internal state. It's the therapist's task to accept and understand these communications, helping the child to explore their emotions fully.

For you as a parent, applying this principle while playing with your child involves fostering a judgment-free environment where your child can openly express their emotions through play. The play setting should become a safe space for your child to display behaviors that reflect their feelings, without the worry of being corrected or directed. It's important for you to show that you are comfortable with a broad spectrum of emotional expressions, recognizing that even less desirable behaviors, such as shouting or pounding on a toy, are part of your child's way of exploring and communicating emotions.

Application example:

Imagine your child is building and then knocking down a block tower repeatedly. Rather than guiding them or asking questions about why they keep knocking it down, you might simply observe and comment, "You're really putting a lot of effort into building that tower and then knocking it down." This way, you're acknowledging what they're doing without directing their response or actions. It creates a supportive and accepting environment, allowing your child to continue their exploration in their own way.

Principle 4: The therapist is alert to recognize the feelings the child is expressing and reflects those feelings back to him in such a manner that he gains insight into his behavior.

In the therapeutic space, the therapist is like a mirror, reflecting the child's emotional expressions back to them. This is a subtle dance of observing not only the child's play but also the feelings that animate it. When a therapist accurately identifies and verbalizes the emotions a child exhibits, it helps the child to develop an emotional vocabulary. This reflective process does not involve interpretation or analysis by the therapist, but rather a simple acknowledgment that helps the child to see their own feelings more clearly. For example, if a child is playing with a toy in a particularly aggressive manner, the therapist might say, "You're playing very intensely with your toy; it looks like there's some angry feelings happening right now." This comment allows the child to consider their own feelings without judgment.

As a parent, you can utilize this principle by becoming attuned to your child's verbal and nonverbal cues and reflecting back the actions and emotions you observe in a supportive manner. It's about providing your children with the words to describe feelings they might not yet fully understand. Remember, the goal is not to solve or correct the emotion, but rather to validate and acknowledge it. This approach gives your child the tools they need to process their own emotions effectively.

Application example:

Imagine your child is playing with a group of toy animals and decides to place one figure apart from the rest, pretending that this toy is crying. As a parent, you can acknowledge this emotional expression by saying, "The toy seems to be crying; it looks pretty sad over there all by itself." By making this observation, you are reflecting the emotion your child is expressing through their play, without trying to guess or ask why the toy is sad. This approach maintains a non-directive stance, allowing your child to explore and express emotions in their own way, while you recognize and validate these expressions.

Principle 5: The therapist maintains a deep respect for the child's ability to solve his own problems if given an opportunity to do so. The responsibility to make choices and institute change is the child's.

The essence of this principle is the trust in the child's natural ability to work through difficulties when provided with a supportive environment. It is about honoring the child's autonomy and facilitating a space where they can engage with and learn from their experiences at their own pace. The therapist's role is not to provide solutions but to respect and reinforce the child's capacity to find their own.

As a parent integrating this principle into playtime, you must consciously hold back from stepping in to solve problems or guide your child's play. It's about allowing your child to lead their own discovery and problem-solving processes. This restraint involves resisting the urge to correct your child's actions or offer solutions, even when you see them struggling or making mistakes. By doing so, you're giving your child the opportunity to learn through their own experiences.

Application example:

Imagine your child is struggling to complete a task, like fitting the right shapes into a puzzle. Your natural inclination might be to guide them. However, embracing this principle means you observe and acknowledge their effort without stepping in. You might comment neutrally, "You're working hard on figuring out where each piece goes." This approach gives your child the space to decide whether to ask for help, try a different strategy on their own, or even to leave the puzzle and move on to another activity. By doing so, you are providing your child with the opportunity to handle frustration and develop problem-solving skills. This reinforces their autonomy and builds confidence in their abilities.

Principle 6: The therapist does not attempt to direct the child's actions or conversation in any manner. The child leads the way; the therapist follows.

The therapist maintains a non-directive approach during sessions, allowing the child to guide the direction of their actions and dialogues. In this method, the therapist plays a passive, supporting role, emphasizing the child's autonomy and choices. The therapist refrains from leading or suggesting specific actions or topics. However, if a child specifically seeks assistance or guidance during play, the therapist offers just enough support to address that immediate need, ensuring they don't overstep or influence the child's inherent direction or discoveries. Essentially, the child is the leader of the session, and the therapist acts as a facilitator, present to assist only when explicitly called upon.

When you are playing with your child, it's crucial for you to let them guide the direction and theme of the play. You should adopt a facilitative role, immersing yourself in your child's imaginative world without trying to direct or influence it. If your child explicitly asks for assistance, then you should offer only the necessary help needed for that specific situation. This approach allows your child to feel in control of their play environment, encouraging creativity and independence.

Application example:

Imagine your child is meticulously arranging a miniature tea set and invites you to join their imaginary feast. Your role in this situation is to be a participant, not a director. Upon joining the circle of stuffed animal guests, you might inquire, "Where would you like me to sit for the tea party?" This allows your child to assert their vision, assigning you a spot and perhaps even a character to play. If your child hands you a tiny, empty cup, play along by asking, "What kind of tea are we having today?" By engaging in this way, you respect your child's creative lead, reinforcing their storytelling skills and decision-making. Your gentle inquiries support the unfolding narrative without overtaking your child's autonomy.

Principle 7: The therapist does not attempt to hurry the therapy along. It is a gradual process and is recognized as such by the therapist.

The essence of this principle lies in the therapist's respect for the natural tempo at which a child progresses through therapy. It's understood that the journey is not to be rushed; the therapist recognizes the gradual nature of emotional healing and development. This patience is crucial, allowing the child to explore their thoughts and feelings without feeling pressured to reach quicker resolutions or insights.

In adhering to this principle, you, as a parent, consciously refrain from pushing your child to explain or elaborate on their feelings before they are ready. You avoid asking pointed or leading questions that might pressure your child into analyzing or sharing their emotions prematurely. This means that even if you are curious or concerned about the feelings behind your child's play, you do not rush them to express those feelings more quickly than they might naturally do so. Instead, you allow your child to reveal emotions at a pace that's comfortable for them, ensuring they do not feel an obligation to provide explanations or insights they have not yet fully formed or understood themselves. By doing so, you create a trusting environment where your child feels secure to express emotions slowly and genuinely, knowing that their personal timing is both respected and supported by you.

Application example:

Imagine your child is drawing a series of pictures that, to you, seem to have a sad theme – maybe they're drawings of a rainy day or people with frowns. As a parent applying this principle, you resist the urge to immediately ask, "Why are all your pictures so sad?" or "Are you feeling unhappy?" Asking these kinds of questions might push your child to analyze or articulate their feelings before they are ready, which could be overwhelming or confusing for them. Instead, you might simply acknowledge the artwork by saying, "I see you've drawn a lot of rain today," or "I notice there are a lot of frowns in your drawings." This approach allows your child to either share more about their feelings or continue their activity without the pressure of having to explain their emotional state. Your role is to be present and attentive, ready to listen and respond if and when your child decides to open up about their emotions. This patient and non-intrusive style gives your child the time they need to process their feelings and communicate them on their own terms.

Principle 8: The therapist establishes only those limitations that are necessary to anchor the therapy to the world of reality and to make the child aware of his responsibility in the relationship.

In therapeutic settings, boundaries are essential, not as constraints, but as grounding elements that link the child's imaginative play to the realities of life. Therapists set limits to reinforce a sense of order and responsibility, making the child aware that their actions within the playroom have meaning. Sessions are timed, usually lasting an hour, to establish consistency and a sense of duration. Children are encouraged to immerse themselves in the creative process, but with the understanding that they must not inflict harm upon themselves, the therapist, or the toys. While normal wear and tear on toys is expected, willfully destructive behavior is not permitted. These rules are not just for the safety of all involved but also to instill an understanding that even in a space dedicated to freedom of expression, responsibility is paramount.

As a parent adopting this principle at home, you would set playtime boundaries at the beginning of your Meaningful Playtime sessions. You'd explain that while this is a special time for play and your child is in charge, some rules still apply. You would clarify that accidents with toys can happen during play, and that's okay, but intentional damage to the toys is not acceptable. The same rule applies to the play setting – for example, painting the walls is not allowed. Another important rule is that harming each other or oneself is not permitted. You'd also outline the session's length, ensuring your child understands the significance of this dedicated time, but also that it has a beginning and an end. Finally, it's crucial for you to convey to your child that while your shared playtime is a special time in the week, it exists alongside the ongoing flow of daily life, which has its own structure and guidelines. Once the play session concludes, you both transition back to the day-to-day world where other rules and responsibilities continue to apply.

Example for Application:

During the first Meaningful Playtime session, you might say to your child: "During our playtime together, we have some important rules to make sure we both stay safe. You can choose any game you want to play, and you can play with the toys in your own way, just remember that we don't break them on purpose. If something breaks by accident, that's okay, it happens! But we will keep our play safe and respectful. The same applies to the room – we won't intentionally make any damage, like pouring paint on the rug or drawing on the walls. We are not allowed to harm ourselves or each other either. Our Meaningful Playtime sessions will be every Friday at 5pm and will last one hour. When our hour of play is up, we'll tidy up and get ready for our other daily tasks, just like we always do. Then, all the rules of normal life will apply again." This clear communication helps your child understand the boundaries of Meaningful Playtime while reinforcing the concept of intentional care and respect for themselves, others, and their environment.

9. The ultimate easy step-by-step guide on how to engage in Meaningful Playtime

As we approach the culmination of our journey through this book, it's time to pivot from theory to practice, translating the insights gained into tangible experiences with your child. The following section will serve as your roadmap, guiding you in creating an environment that fosters connection, expression, and growth. We'll delve into crafting an inviting play space, thoughtfully selecting toys that spark creativity and emotional expression, and establishing a rhythm for your Meaningful Playtime sessions that resonates with the tempo of your family life. With these preparations in place, you'll be ready to embark on the first play session, setting the stage for meaningful and quality playtime with your child.

1. Label your play sessions: Meaningful Playtime

It's crucial to give a unique name to the quality time you will spend playing with your child. I have labeled them 'Meaningful Playtime' in this book, but you can choose any label you prefer: some other ideas are 'Cozy Playtime', 'Comfy Playtime', 'Shared Playtime', and so on. By labeling these sessions you help your child to understand that this is not just regular play. It's a dedicated time for connection and expression, distinctly different from their other daily activities. This term becomes a special code between you two, signifying that during these sessions the usual rules of play are set aside. It is a time when they can fully lead the way in play, with you there to support and listen, fully immersed in their world. Giving these sessions a specific label not only helps to set them apart in your child's mind but also emphasizes their importance in your family's routine.

2. Introduce Meaningful Playtime to your child

When the moment feels right, invite your child to have a chat with you about a new idea you're excited to share with them. Explain that you've been thinking about how wonderful it would be to have a special time set aside just for the two of you to play together. Describe Meaningful Playtime as a time when they can lead the play in any way they choose while you give them your full attention and participate in their world of fun and imagination.

Express to them that this will be a unique time for bonding and enjoyment, and you're looking forward to seeing where their creativity takes you both. Emphasize that this play will be different because it's a time dedicated to just the two of you, without any interruptions or distractions. If they show interest, that's your cue to decide together when to schedule your first Meaningful Playtime session. Agree on a day and time that works for both of you, marking it as an important date on your calendar. This shared decision-making will help your child feel valued and excited about the special times ahead.

3. Prepare the play setting

In preparing the play setting for truly enriching Meaningful Playtime, it's important to consider the environment and the choice of toys. Following the recommendations of Landreth (1993), the space should be comfortable and inviting, without the need for a specialized playroom. Any consistent, quiet area where your child feels at ease is ideal. Landreth emphasizes the importance of selecting toys that are not only enjoyable but also facilitate the expression of feelings and experiences. He suggests opting for simple, adaptable toys that encourage creative expression and role-playing. These toys should enable your child to:

- Reenact familiar scenarios and explore roles.
- Explore a range of emotions.
- Practice understanding limits.
- Dive into various types of play, from imaginative to physical.
- Communicate non-verbally.
- Play freely without complex rules.

List of toys

Here is a categorized list of recommended items to include in your play setting: the toys and materials suggested below serve merely as examples to inspire your selection for Meaningful Playtime. While it's beneficial to have a variety of items from each category to enrich the play experience, there's no expectation to acquire everything listed. The aim is not to amass toys, but to curate a diverse collection that resonates with your child and fits the purpose of these sessions. Feel free to use what you already have at home and consider adding new items that you believe would complement your child's play. Each child is unique, and their playtime should reflect their individual interests and developmental stage. The following suggestions are intended to spark ideas and provide a starting point for creating an environment that's conducive to expressive, imaginative, and meaningful play. It is by no means expected that all the toys and materials listed below are to be included in the Meaningful Playtime space. See what you have at home or what you would like to buy, and start with that.

Artistic Expression		
• Crayons • Watercolor paints • Newsprint • Blunt scissors • Colored pencils • Markers • Glue sticks • Glitter • Stickers	• Transparent tape • Clay or playdough • Finger paints • Sketchbooks • Stencils and stamps • Craft paper (various colors and textures) • Fabric scraps • Beads and string for jewelry-making • Pipe cleaners	• Foam sheets • Yarn • Sidewalk chalk • Sequins • Feathers • Pom poms • Wooden craft sticks • Googly eyes • Ribbons
Nurturing and Care		
• Nursing bottle • Dolls with various clothes • Stuffed animals • Dollhouse with furniture • Play dishes and cups • Plastic food items • Baby blankets • Toy medical kit	• Miniature strollers or prams • Toy highchairs • Miniature beds or cradles for dolls • Child-sized aprons • Toy bathtub set • Diaper changing kit for dolls • Toy kitchen appliances (like a blender or toaster) • Gardening tools set	• Toy cleaning set (broom, mop, dustpan) • Picnic set • Child's tea set • Play tool set • Dress-up clothes (for role-playing different caregivers) • Pet care play set • Pretend makeup set • Toy grocery cart • Doll carrier or sling

Adventure and Role-Play		
• Dart gun • Handcuffs • Toy soldiers • Dress-up costumes • Lone Ranger-type mask • Superhero capes and masks • Knight armor and shields • Magic wands and wizard hats	• Spy gear (like toy binoculars and walkie-talkies) • Police officer costume set • Firefighter gear • Astronaut helmet and suit • Doctor's coat and stethoscope • Princess dresses and tiaras • Animal costumes (like lions, tigers, etc.) • Pirate hats and eye patches	• Fairy wings and tutus • Ninja accessories • Toy swords and shields • Cowboy hats and boots • Dinosaur figures and playsets • Race car driver suit and helmet • Mermaid tails and crowns • Medieval castle playsets
Creative Construction		
• Clay or Play-Doh with tools • Magnetic building blocks • Wooden blocks • Popsicle sticks • Pipe cleaners • Lego or other interlocking bricks • Cardboard building blocks • Lincoln logs	• K'Nex sets • Foam building blocks • Tinkertoy sets • Gears and wheels sets • Marble run sets • Construction paper (for making paper models) • Straw connectors • Wooden train tracks and trains	• Building planks (like Kapla or KEVA planks) • Snap circuits (for older children) • Jigsaw puzzles • Plastic tool set • Model airplane or car kits • Sandcastle tools (for sandbox play) • Robotics kits (for older kids) • Craft sticks and glue (for creating structures) • Bead and string kits (for making structures and jewelry)

Physical Play		
• Small airplane • Small cars and trucks • Nerf ball • Inflatable vinyl punching bag • Softballs and bats • Jump ropes • Hula hoops	• Mini trampoline (with safety net) • Indoor bowling set • Bean bags • Small pop-up soccer goals and soft soccer ball • Indoor basketball hoop with foam ball • Balance boards • Twister game	• Soft play mats for gymnastics or yoga • Indoor hopscotch mat • Ring toss game • Floor puzzles (large pieces) • Velcro dart board • Inflatable tumbling rolls • Stretch bands for simple stretching exercises
Communication and Social Interaction		
• Play telephone • Walkie-talkies • Hand puppets • Bendable doll family • Dollhouse with family figures	• Simple card games • Emotion flashcards • Storytelling dice • Role-playing game kits • Cooperative board games	• Play money and cash register • Toy mailboxes with letters and stamps • Conversation starter cards • Multiplayer puzzle games • Toy microphones for singing and storytelling • Pretend play restaurant or store kit
Symbolic Play Kits		
• Doctor sets • Kitchen sets • Hairdresser sets • Tool sets • Gardening sets • Supermarket checkout set • Firefighter kit • Police officer role play set	• Tea party set • Astronaut gear • Veterinarian kit • Ice cream shop set • Magic trick set • Pirate adventure kit • Fairy tale dress-up set • School teacher play set	• Bakery play set • Construction worker kit • Train conductor set • Dinosaur explorer kit • Mail carrier set • Camping adventure gear • Fishing play set • Race car driver kit • Zookeeper role play set

Miniature World Recreation		
• Sand tray with miniature tools • Miniature animals and families • Miniature vehicles • Small figurines of people and fantasy characters • Miniature trees and plants • Dollhouses with detailed furniture • Tiny road and railway sets • Small-scale building blocks	• Miniature sports fields and accessories • Toy soldier sets • Miniature farm set with barn and animals • Tiny boats and ships • Small-scale airport with planes • Miniature theme park set • Little city play mats with roads and buildings • Miniature castle with knights and dragons	• Tiny space station and astronauts • Microscopic science lab set • Mini zoo with various animal figurines • Little fairy garden kit • Miniature camping site with tents and campfire • Small beach scene with umbrellas and chairs • Miniature circus set with performers and animals • Tiny dinosaur world with volcanoes and fossils

Organizing the play setting for consistency and comfort

As we've discussed, the most important aspect of the play setting for Meaningful Playtime is that it's a consistent, quiet area where your child feels safe and relaxed. If you have the luxury of a dedicated playroom or a specific section of your child's bedroom, keep the toys organized there. On the other hand, if your chosen area doesn't have storage, like a shared space in your living room, simply prepare the same selection of toys in the same arrangement before each session.

The key is consistency – the play area should be the same from session to session, as should the toy setup.

Categorizing the toys and creating distinct zones for different types of play – such as areas for artistic expression, nurturing, adventure, and so on – can help provide structure and familiarity. If you're setting up before each Meaningful Playtime session, consider taking a photo of the setup during your initial session. This will serve as a handy reference to recreate the environment, ensuring each playtime feels familiar to your child, providing a sense of security and routine that's crucial for their comfort and willingness to engage fully in the play experience.

4. Decide on a routine for meaningful playtime

Just as consistency in the play setting forms a bedrock of comfort and reliability for your child, so too does a regular schedule. It's crucial to establish a routine that your child can anticipate and look forward to. Decide on a day, time, and frequency for your Meaningful Playtime sessions and commit to this schedule. Whether it's every Saturday morning at 10am for an hour, or bi-weekly for a longer or shorter duration, the regularity will foster a sense of structure and expectation.

This routine not only helps your child feel secure in knowing when they'll have your undivided attention, but it also enhances the overall impact and progression of the sessions. A predictable routine ensures that Meaningful Playtime becomes a staple of your child's week, something that they can look forward to and cherish. As you both grow accustomed to this rhythm, you'll likely find that the anticipation of these sessions adds an extra layer of excitement and joy to your time together. You will tell your child about the regularity of the sessions during your first Meaningful Playtime session.

5. Learn beforehand how to set up limits

When embracing the concept of Meaningful Playtime, it's essential to blend the freedom of child-led play with a layer of safety and respect. You may feel a twinge of concern at the thought of completely unstructured play. What if your child's imagination leads them toward something less safe? Here's where setting gentle yet clear boundaries becomes crucial – it provides structure and reassurance for both you and your child.

Therefore, before diving into Meaningful Playtime it's important to lay down a few simple rules. This isn't about limiting fun; it's about creating a safe space where your child knows that their well-being is a priority. In your first session, you'll want to share these guidelines:

1. We take care to avoid hurting ourselves.
2. We don't break toys on purpose.
3. We don't damage the play area on purpose.
4. Our Meaningful Playtime lasts for the agreed duration – long enough to have a world of fun, but finite, so we know when it's time to wrap up and return to our day.

An example of how the rules could be introduced is:

"During Meaningful Playtime together, you get to decide how we play with the toys, but we do have a few important rules to keep us safe and take care of our play space:

1. We don't harm ourselves: This means we won't do anything that could hurt you or me.
2. We don't break toys on purpose: Sometimes toys break by accident, and that's okay. But we should try not to break them intentionally.
3. We don't damage the play setting on purpose: We should take care of the area where we play.
4. The sessions will last one hour: Once our hour is up, we'll need to stop, even if we're having a lot of fun. It's part of how we learn to manage our playtime together. Afterward, we'll move on with the rest of our daily activities."

Some parents may find it helpful to introduce a rule about tidying up before the end of the session. This can be a useful way to symbolically close the playtime, allowing your child to wrap up any emotions or experiences that emerged during the session. It also serves as a gentle transition, helping them prepare to return to their daily routine in a calm and collected manner. To facilitate this, it's a good idea to give your child a heads-up when there are about 10 minutes left. This way, they can begin to tidy up at their own pace, which not only teaches responsibility but also helps them process the transition from playtime back to regular activities. The rule could be introduced as follows:

5. "We tidy up before the end of the session: With about 10 minutes left, I'll give you a little reminder that it's almost time to finish. Then we can start putting everything back together. It's important for us to leave our play space neat and tidy, so next time we come to play everything is ready and waiting for us. This way, we can jump right into having fun again!"

Address rule-breaking

There might be times during Meaningful Playtime when your child doesn't follow the rules you both agreed on. This could happen for various reasons; for example, they may have forgotten the rules, or they might be testing boundaries to see how you respond. It's natural for this to feel challenging for you as a parent. However, managing these situations can be made easier by following some steps outlined by Landreth (1991). These steps provide a clear and effective way to address rule-breaking during playtime, helping to maintain a safe and enjoyable environment for both you and your child:

1. **Recognize their feelings:** Start by acknowledging your child's emotions. Say something like, "I see you really seem to be enjoying your painting right now!"

2. **State the rule:** Remind them of the agreed rules in a clear, gentle manner. For instance, "Remember, we don't damage the play area on purpose, so we should not be painting on the wall."

3. **Offer other choices:** Suggest acceptable alternatives to guide them back within the boundaries. You could say, "Why don't we get your drawing book or some paper for your painting?"

If your child continues to test the limits after a reminder:

Provide consequences: Explain the consequences of not following the rules, ensuring your tone remains calm but firm. For example, "If you continue painting on the wall, we'll need to put away the paints for today or end our play session early."

Remember, the goal is not to punish but to guide them back to safe and respectful play. It's also a learning opportunity for them to understand the importance of following rules.

6. Learn beforehand effective ways for closing each session

For closing each Meaningful Playtime session effectively, it's vital to understand the importance of this phase. These sessions can be emotionally intense for your child, as they might be navigating and processing a range of feelings, including some challenging ones. This emotional exploration is a positive sign, indicating that the sessions are serving their purpose in facilitating emotional expression and processing. However, precisely because of the depth of these emotions, it's crucial to transition gently back to everyday life.

Closing the session thoughtfully allows your child to gradually conclude their emotional journey for the day and re-enter their regular routine in a more settled emotional state. As discussed earlier, one effective method to facilitate this transition is to establish a rule for tidying up the play area. This physical act of organizing the toys and materials used during play can symbolically represent the child 'putting away' their emotions, helping them to compartmentalize and process their experiences.

To make this transition smooth, it's helpful to give your child a heads-up about the session nearing its end. A 10-minute warning lets them know it's time to start wrapping up their play. You might want to offer another reminder when there are 5 minutes left. This gives them ample time to mentally prepare for the end of the session and start the process of tidying up, whether it's the physical space or their emotional state.

Even if you choose not to include tidying up as part of the closing ritual, it's still essential to signal the approaching end of the playtime. This helps your child mentally prepare for the transition from the special world of play back to their everyday life. It's a gentle way to bring them back to the present while acknowledging and respecting the emotional journey they've just undertaken.

7. The first session

As you embark on the inaugural Meaningful Playtime session with your child, a few key elements are essential to ensure its success. This first session lays the foundation for future interactions and sets the tone for how these playtimes will unfold. Here's how to approach it:

1. **Clarify the concept of child-centered play:** Start by reinforcing the concept you discussed with your child earlier. Emphasize that during Meaningful Playtime they are in complete control. Whether they want to engage in imaginative play, enjoy a quiet moment, or embark on an active game, it's entirely up to them. Explain that their role is to lead and yours is to follow, whether that means actively participating or simply being present as an observer. Stress the fact that their choices are respected and valued, whether they wish to play, rest, or engage in any other activity within the play area. Assure them of your undivided attention, free from any distractions like phone calls or household chores.

    Here's an example on how you could introduce this:

    > "Remember when we talked about starting our Meaningful Playtime together? Well, it's now our time, and I want you to know that this time is all about what you want to do. Whether you feel like building a castle, just sitting quietly, or maybe running around pretending to be an astronaut, it's totally your choice. I'm here to join in on whatever you decide, or just to watch and enjoy seeing you have fun. This time is special because it's yours – you get to decide everything. If you want to play with your toys in

a new way, that's great. If you'd rather just sit and talk, or even if you don't feel like talking, that's okay too. My job is just to be with you and to be part of whatever you want to do. And don't worry, I won't be answering any phone calls or doing anything else – I'm all yours for this time. This is our special time to play or just be together, however you choose."

2. **Establish the Meaningful Playtime schedule:** Take a moment to share with your child the specifics of your planned Meaningful Playtime sessions. Discuss the day, time, duration, and frequency of these sessions, ensuring your child understands and agrees with this schedule. As highlighted in point 4 of our guide, creating a consistent routine is key. This consistency forms a reliable foundation, offering your child a sense of security and something joyful to anticipate. It's about building a regular, special slot in your lives that's dedicated solely to exploring, playing, and connecting with each other. Let them know that this time is reserved just for the two of you, a special period where you both can connect, play, and learn together, undisturbed by the outside world.

3. **Introduce the boundaries:** Gently remind them of the rules discussed earlier. Explain that while they have the freedom to lead the play, certain boundaries are in place to ensure safety and respect for both of you and the play environment. This is crucial to creating a safe and trusting atmosphere for play.

Check point 5 of this guide for an example on how to introduce the rules.

4. **Outline the session's ending:** Inform them about the process of ending the session. Explain that you will give them a 10-minute and then a 5-minute notice before the session ends. If you've decided to include tidying up as part of the closing routine, explain to them that this is the time to start wrapping up and organizing the toys and materials used during play. This helps in mentally preparing them to transition from the playtime back to their regular daily routine.

5. **Transition back to routine:** Make it clear that once Meaningful Playtime concludes, the norms and rules of everyday life resume. This helps to demarcate the special session from regular daily activities, reinforcing the structure and routine in their lives.

6. **Time to play:** Once you've shared all the crucial details of the first session with your child, and if there's still time remaining, you can delve into the actual Meaningful Playtime. Recall everything you've absorbed from this book, particularly Axline's principles of child-centered play. Immerse yourself in your child's world, allowing them to take the lead. Embrace this opportunity to connect, understand, and enjoy the unique world your child creates during these sessions. Remember, this is as much a journey for you as it is for your child – an opportunity to see the world through their eyes and strengthen your bond. Be mindful of the time, and as you approach

the final 10 minutes of the session, gently remind your child.

8. Following sessions

In your future Meaningful Playtime sessions, you and your child can dive right into the fun since they'll already know the ropes. This is your chance to really put into practice everything we've discussed in this book. Especially focus on embracing Axline's principles of child-centered play. Let your child lead the way in these sessions. They're the captain of this ship, and you're there to enjoy the journey with them.

Remember the plan you set up in your first session about when and how long your playtimes would be. Keeping up with this schedule is really important. Consistency helps make these play sessions a special and expected part of both your lives.

As you embark on these Meaningful Playtime adventures, cherish each moment. These sessions are more than just play; they're building blocks for a deeper bond and understanding between you and your child. Enjoy the journey, treasure the discoveries, and watch the magical bond between you both grow stronger with each playful moment.

Brief example of a meaningful playtime interaction

Daughter (age 5): (Picking up a toy airplane) "Look, Mommy, my airplane is flying really high!"

Mother: "Wow, it's flying so high!"

(The daughter then suddenly drops the airplane and looks sad.)

Daughter: "But... but it crashed. It's broken now."

Mother: "Oh no, your airplane crashed. That seems really upsetting."

Daughter: (Nods and starts fixing the airplane) "I can fix it. I need to make it better."

Mother: "You're working hard to fix it. You really want to make it better."

(The daughter manages to put the toy back together and looks happy.)

Daughter: "I fixed it! It can fly again!"

Mother: "You did it! You fixed the airplane. Now it can fly again. That must feel really good."

Daughter: "Yes! Now it won't crash. It's strong."

Mother: "Your airplane is strong. You figured out how to fix it and make it strong."

(The daughter smiles and continues to play, visibly proud and more engaged.)

In this interaction, the mother lets her daughter lead the play, offering support and reflection without directing the play. She acknowledges her daughter's emotions and efforts, fostering a sense of empowerment and understanding.

10. Meaningful Playtime with babies and toddlers

Expanding on the concept of Meaningful Playtime for babies and toddlers, it's important to adapt the approach to fit their developmental stage and understanding. While they might not grasp the idea of leading play or following rules, there are still effective ways to engage in meaningful play with them. Piaget's Play Stages indicate that symbolic play becomes more significant from around age two, and it's around age three when child-led play sessions, as described in this book, are most effective. However, this doesn't mean you can't engage in meaningful play with younger children. Let's explore some adaptations for Meaningful Playtime with younger children:

1. **Adapting to baby-centered Meaningful Playtime:** Babies and toddlers are mostly in the stage of functional play, so your approach will differ. You might set up a playmat with age-appropriate toys and observe as they explore. Your role is to be present, observe, and engage when your child shows interest or initiates interaction. If they interact with you, like offering a toy, respond to their cues while maintaining a child-centered approach. This can include simple actions like smiling back, gently talking, or handing a toy back when they reach out to you. Basically, mirror their expressions and sounds to show understanding and connection. But let them figure things out on

their own, resisting the temptation to show them how to play with a toy. It's important to resist the urge to direct their play. This approach fosters independence and confidence in their abilities to explore and discover.

2. **Adapting the introduction of rules:** When having Meaningful Playtime with babies there is no need to introduce the rules during the first session, as they won't understand them. Your role will be to keep the basic rules in mind and take action to protect your child, yourself, and the play setting when needed. In the case of toddlers, they might not understand and remember the rules if explained all at once in the first session, but you can introduce them as needed. This can be a learning process, and you can use Landreth's guidelines from point 5 of this guideline to address rule-breaking for introducing rules for toddlers and young children. For instance, if a toddler is about to paint on the wall, acknowledge their feeling "I see you are enjoying painting the wall", gently introduce the rule "We should make sure that we don't damage the play area on purpose so we should not be painting on the wall," and offer an alternative, like painting on paper "Let's use this paper to paint on it instead."

3. **Adapting the closure of sessions:** With babies, you won't need a formal closing, but as your child grows, you can start introducing the concept. Notify them when the end of the session is approaching, allowing them to mentally prepare. This helps them wrap up their play and emotions, transitioning back to daily routines.

4. **Introducing the full concept of Meaningful Playtime around the age of 3:** As children reach the age where symbolic play becomes more prevalent, you can start introducing the full concept of Meaningful Playtime as described in this book. This includes explaining that they are in charge of the play, can decide how to play, and that it's okay if they sometimes don't feel like playing at all.

5. **Consistent play setting:** Regardless of age, ensure the play setting is consistent, quiet, and comfortable. Adapt it to suit their developmental needs as they grow, providing toys and materials that encourage exploration and expression appropriate for their age.

6. **Embracing consistency in playtime:** Consistency is a cornerstone of Meaningful Playtime, vital for children of all ages. Start with manageable time slots that align with your child's age and attention span. For very young children, even 15 minutes of dedicated playtime can be significant. As your child grows and their developmental needs evolve, you can adjust the duration accordingly. This regular commitment to playtime establishes a dependable routine, offering your child a stable and nurturing environment where they feel secure and valued.

11. The adventure begins: Wrapping up our guide

As you embark on this journey of Meaningful Playtime with your child, you're stepping into a role that is both profound and transformative. This book has equipped you with the understanding and tools to engage with your child in a way that's deeply enriching and nurturing. Remember, the essence of Meaningful Playtime isn't found in perfection but in the genuine effort and connection you offer. It's about creating a space where your child feels seen, heard, and valued, a place where their imagination and emotions can explore freely, guided by their own ideas and inclinations.

This practice may initially feel unfamiliar or even awkward for some. The idea of fully immersing oneself in a child's play can be challenging, perhaps evoking feelings of self-consciousness or uncertainty. Yet, with time and dedication, this process will become more natural. You'll discover the joys and insights that come from seeing the world through your child's eyes. Your willingness to engage, to listen, and to be present, is a gift of immeasurable value to your child, and the impact of this gift will resonate far beyond these play sessions.

Meaningful Playtime it's a journey into the heart of your child's world. It's an opportunity to forge deeper bonds, to understand their unique perspective, and to aid them in navigating their emotions and experiences. Whether your child is thriving or facing challenges, these sessions are a potent tool for their development and well-being.

As you close this book and begin your own Meaningful Playtime adventures, hold onto the knowledge that your efforts, patience, and presence are making a significant difference in your child's life. You are helping to shape a world for them where they feel confident, understood, and loved. So, embrace each session with an open heart, a listening ear, and a readiness to explore. The journey you're about to embark on is one of discovery, growth, and joy – for both you and your child.

Bibliography

American Psychological Association (2017). Cognitive and social skills to expect from 3 to 5 years. Retrieved: June 20, 2023 from https://www.apa.org/act/resources/fact-sheets/development-5-years

Anthony, M. (2019). Cognitive development in 0-2-year-olds. Retrieved: June 10, 2023 from https://www.scholastic.com/parents/family-life/creativity-and-critical-thinking/development-milestones/cognitive-development-0-2-year-olds.html

Anthony, M. (n.d.). Cognitive development in 3-5-year-olds. Retrieved: July 9, 2023, from https://www.scholastic.com/parents/family-life/creativity-and-critical-thinking/development-milestones/cognitive-development-3-5-year-olds.html

Anthony, M. (2019a). Cognitive development in 8-10-year-olds. Retrieved: April 3, 2023 from https://www.scholastic.com/parents/family-life/creativity-and-critical-thinking/development-milestones/cognitive-development-8-10-year-olds.html

Archer, C., & Burnell, A. (2003). *Trauma, Attachment and Family Permanence*. London: Jessica Kingsley Publishers.

Axline, V. (1947). *Play Therapy: The Inner Dynamics of Childhood*. Cambridge, MA: Houghton Mifflin.

Axline, V. (1964). 'Recognition and reflection of feelings', in Haworth, M. (ed.) Child Psychotherapy. New York: Basic Books.

Axline, V. (1964a). *Dibs: In Search of Self*. New York: Ballantine and Harmondsworth: Penguin.

Axline, V. (1989). *Play therapy*. Boston: Houghton Mifflin and Edinburgh: Churchill Livingstone.

Bailey, J., & Davis, T. (2018). Superheroes and play therapy: The perfect imaginary combination. Counseling Today. Retrieved: May 5, 2023 from https://ct.counseling.org/2018/07/superheroes-and-play-therapy-the-perfect-imaginary-combination/

Barn, R. (Ed.) (1999). *Working with Black Children and Adolescents in Need*. London: BAAF.

Benefits of play therapy: How play rewires the brain? (2019). Building Better Brains. Retrieved: December 12, 2022 from https://buildingbetterbrains.com.au/how-play-rewires-the-brain/

Bentovim, A. (1977). 'The role of play in psycho-therapeutic work with children and their families', in B. Tizard & D. Harvey (Eds.), *The Biology of Play*. London: Heinemann.

Bowlby, J. (1969). *Attachment: Volume One of the Attachment and Loss Series*. London: The Hogarth Press and the Institute of Psycho-Analysis.

Bowlby, J. (1973). *Separation: Anxiety and Anger: Volume Two of the Attachment and Loss Series*. London: The Hogarth Press and the Institute of Psycho-Analysis.

Bowlby, J. (1980). *Loss: Sadness and Depression: Volume Three of the Attachment and Loss Series*. London: The Hogarth Press and the Institute of Psycho-Analysis.

Bowlby, J. (1988). *A Secure Base: Clinical Applications of Attachment Theory*. London: Routledge.

Bradley, C. (1999). 'Making sense of symbolic communication', in A. Hardwick & J. Woodhead (Eds.), *Loving, Hating and Survival*. London: Arena/Ashgate.

Bratton, S., Ray, D., Rhine, T., & Jones, L. (2005). 'The efficacy of play therapy with children: A meta-analytic review of treatment outcomes'. *Professional Psychology: Research and Practice, 36*(4), 376-390.

Bruner, J. S., Jolly, A., & Sylva, K. (Eds.) (1976). *Play: Its Role in Development and Evolution*. Harmondsworth: Penguin.

Bzostek, S. H., & Berger, L. M. (2017). Family structure experiences and socioemotional child development during the first nine years of life: Examining heterogeneity by family structure at birth. Demography, 54(2), 513-540. Retrieved: November 14, 2022 from https://doi.org/10.1007/s13524-017-0563-5

Carroll, J. (1998). *Introduction to Therapeutic Play*. Oxford: Blackwell.

Dyke, S. (1984). 'Letting go: a psychotherapist's view of endings'. *Maladjustment and Therapeutic Education, 2*(1), 52-63.

Elkind, D. (2001). *The Hurried Child: Growing Up Too Fast Too Soon* (3rd ed.). Cambridge, MA: Perseus Publishing.

Erikson, E. H. (1965). *Childhood and society*. New York: Norton; Harmondsworth: Penguin.

Erikson, E. H. (1976). 'Play and actuality', in J. Bruner, A. Jolly & K. Sylva, *Play - Its Role in Development and Evolution*. Harmondsworth: Penguin.

Elmore, L. B. (2012). Role play. Retrieved: August 10, 2022 from https://ablconnect.harvard.edu/role-play-research

Freud, A. (1936). *The Ego and the Mechanisms of Defence*. London: Hogarth Press.

Gardner, R. A. (1971). *Therapeutic Communication with Children: The Mutual Storytelling Technique*. New York: Science House.

Garvey, C. (1997). *Play*. Cambridge, MA: Harvard University Press.

Gerhardt, S. (2004). *Why Love Matters: How Affection Shapes a Baby's Brain*. London: Routledge.

Gil, E. (1991). *The Healing Power of Play: Working with Abused Children*. New York: Guilford Press.

Gil, E. (2010). *Helping Abused and Traumatized Children: Integrating Directive and Nondirective Approaches*. New York, NY: Guilford Press.

Ginott, H. (1965). *Between Parent and Child*. New York: Macmillan.

Hashmi, S., Vanderwert, R. E., Price, H., & Gerson, S. (2020). Exploring the Benefits of Doll Play Through Neuroscience. Frontiers in Human Neuroscience, 14. Retrieved: September 10, 2022, from https://www.researchgate.net/publication/344439941_Exploring_the_Benefits_of_Doll_Play_Through_Neuroscience

Haworth, M. (Ed.). (1964). *Child Psychotherapy*. New York, NY: Basic Books.

Hirsh-Pasek, K., & Golinkoff, R. M. (2003). *Einstein Never Used Flash Cards: How Our Children Really Learn – And Why They Need to Play More and Memorize Less*. Emmaus, PA: Rodale Inc.

Holmes, J. (1996). *Attachment, Intimacy, and Autonomy*. London: Routledge.

Holt, J. (1967). *How Children Learn*. New York: Pitman.

Hughes, D. (2000). *Facilitating Developmental Attachment: The Road to Emotional Recovery and Behavioral Change in Foster and Adopted Children*. Jason Aronson.

Jennings, S. (1999). *Introduction to Developmental Play Therapy*. London: Jessica Kingsley Publishers.

Jernberg, A., & Booth, P. (1999). *Theraplay: Helping Parents and Children Build Better Relationships through Attachment-based Play*. San Francisco: Jossey-Bass.

Klein, C. (1977). *How it Feels to Be a Child*. New York: Harper and Row.

Landreth, G. L. (1993). Child-centered play therapy. *Elementary School Guidance & Counseling, Special Issue on Counseling and Children's Play, 28*(1). Retrieved: September 15, 2023, from https://www.jstor.org/stable/i40109110

Landreth, G. L. (2012). *Play Therapy: The Art of the Relationship* (3rd ed.). New York, NY: Routledge.

Lilly, J., & Krull, T. (2015). Play Therapy makes a difference. Association for Play Therapy. Retrieved: July 5, 2023 from https://www.a4pt.org/page/PTMakesADifference/Play-Therapy-Makes-a-Difference.htm

Mackliff, D. (2018). Play therapy: A safe environment mentally and physically. Health, Brain, and Neuroscience. Retrieved: October 28, 2022, from https://yourbrain.health/play-therapy/

McMahon, L. (2009). *The Handbook of Play Therapy and Therapeutic Play*. 2nd ed. East Sussex: Routledge.

Moustakas, C. E. (1959). *Psychotherapy with Children*. New York: Ballantine.

Moustakas, C. E. (1973). *Children in Play Therapy*. New York: Jason Aronson.

Piaget, J. (1951). *Play, Dreams and Imitation in Childhood*. London: Routledge and Kegan Paul.

Piaget, J. (1963). *The Origins of Intelligence in Children*. New York, NY: W. W. Norton & Company.

Piaget, J. (1962). *Play, Dreams, and Imitation in Childhood*. New York: Norton.

Piaget, J., & Inhelder, B. (1969). *The Psychology of the Child*. New York, NY: Basic Books.

Lowenfeld, M. (1967). *Play in Childhood*. New York: John Wiley.

Oaklander, V. (1988). *Windows to Our Children: A Gestalt Therapy Approach to Children and Adolescents*. Moab, UT: Real People Press.

Office of the United Nations High Commissioner for Human Rights. (1989). Convention on the Rights of the Child. General Assembly Resolution 44/25 of 20 November 1989. Retrieved: August 14, 2023, from https://www.ohchr.org/en/instruments-mechanisms/instruments/convention-rights-child

Schaefer, C. (Ed.) (1976). *Therapeutic Use of Child's Play*. New York: Jason Aronson.

Schaefer, C. E. (Ed.) (2003). *Foundations of Play Therapy*. Hoboken, NJ: John Wiley & Sons.

Schaefer, C. E. (Ed.) (2004). *The Handbook of Play Therapy*. Hoboken, NJ: John Wiley & Sons.

Singer, J. (1973). *The Child's World of Make-Believe*. New York: Academic Press.

VanFleet, R., Sywulak, A. E., & Sniscak, C. C. (2010). *Child-Centered Play Therapy*. New York, NY: Guilford Press.

Winnicott, D. W. (1964). *The Child, The Family, and The Outside World*. Harmondsworth: Penguin Books.

Winnicott, D. W. (1971). *Playing and Reality*. London: Tavistock Publications.

Winnicott, D. W. (1971). *Therapeutic Consultation in Child Psychiatry*. New York: Basic Books.

Winnicott, D. W. (1989). *Psycho-Analytic Explorations*. Cambridge, MA: Harvard University Press.

www.ingramcontent.com/pod-product-compliance
Lightning Source LLC
Chambersburg PA
CBHW030848090426
42737CB00009B/1146